75p

JOSEPH OF ARIMATHEA
AT GLASTONBURY

ST. JOSEPH OF ARIMATHEA
AT GLASTONBURY

or

THE APOSTOLIC CHURCH OF BRITAIN

by

THE REV. LIONEL SMITHETT LEWIS, M.A.
late Vicar of Glastonbury

JAMES CLARKE & CO. LTD
33 STORE STREET, LONDON, W.C.1

This edition first published 1955
Reprinted October 1955
Reprinted February 1958

Printed in Great Britain at the St Ann's Press
Park Road, Altrincham

AN OLD GLASTONBURY COLLECT
(*Translated*)

ALMIGHTY, everlasting God, Who didst entrust Thy most blessed servant, Joseph, to take down the lifeless body of Thine Only-Begotten Son from the Cross, and to perform the due offices of humanity, hasten, we pray Thee, that we, who devotedly recall His memory, may feel the help of Thine accustomed pity, through the same, Our Lord. Amen.

THE GLASTONBURY HYMN

AND did those feet in ancient time
    Walk upon England's mountains green?
And was the Holy Lamb of God
    On England's pleasant pastures seen?
And did the Countenance Divine
    Shine forth upon our clouded hills?
And was Jerusalem builded here
    Among those dark Satanic mills?

Bring me my bow of burning gold!
    Bring me my arrows of desire!
Bring me my spear! O clouds unfold!
    Bring me my Chariot of Fire!
I will not cease from mental fight,
    Nor shall my sword sleep in my hand,
Till I have built Jerusalem
    In England's green and pleasant land.

WILLIAM BLAKE, 1757–1827

This hymn, which is founded upon the Glastonbury Tradition, was specially loved and commended to his people by His late Majesty, King George V.

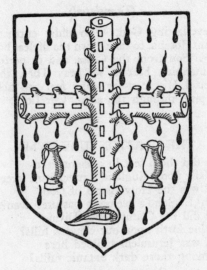

ARMS ACCREDITED TO ST. JOSEPH

FOREWORD TO THE SEVENTH EDITION

by

THE RIGHT REV. THE LORD BISHOP OF BATH AND WELLS

I GLADLY write a Foreword to this 7th Edition of *St. Joseph of Arimathea at Glastonbury*. Mr. Lewis has spent many years of research on this particular tradition, and this Edition of his book incorporates the fruits of his recent work. I hope it may help many to a better appreciation of the place which Glastonbury has in the unfolding of our Christian tradition in England.

WILLIAM BATH: ET WELL:

THE PALACE,
   WELLS, SOMERSET.
June 11, 1953.

NOTE

OWING to the Author's death it has not
been possible to trace all the correspon-
dents to whom he was indebted for
information. If any material incor-
porated in the book is without correct
acknowledgment, or permission has not
been sought and obtained, the Author's
widow apologizes for the seeming dis-
courtesy, which was unavoidable in the
circumstances.

CONTENTS

CONTENTS

ILLUSTRATIONS

ILLUSTRATIONS

CHAPTER I

ANTIQUITY OF GLASTONBURY

AND

ORIGIN OF THE NATIONAL CHURCH

GLASTONBURY has been successively previously called Ynnis-witrin, Isle of Avilion, and Isle of Avalon. John Harding in his Chronicle (temp. Edw. IV) says that it was also constantly called Mewtryen or Mewtryne.[1] But the well-known names are Ynnis-witryn, Avalon, and Glastonbury. Ynnis-witryn is generally supposed to be crystal or glassy isle; Isle of Avilion, isle of departed spirits; Isle of Avalon, isle of apples (the latter being a Saxon corruption of Avilion), and certainly the place excels in apples. It is not strictly correct to pronounce the *t* in Glastonbury, and it has often been spelt Glassenbury. If the usual interpretation of Ynnis Witryn, Glassy or Crystal Isle be accepted, the *en* in Glassenbury may well be *ynnis* or *ennis*, and Glassen a muddled corruption of Ynnis (isle), Witryn (crystal), with the Saxon *bury* or borough tacked on. Such jumbles of different languages do take place in English place names. For instance some three miles from Glastonbury are West Pennard and West Pennard Hill. *Pen* means hill, and *ard* means hill, and so when we say West Pennard Hill we are using three languages to call it

[1] It is rather interesting that Melchinus Avalonius, a prophet, poet, historian, and astronomer (Maelgwyn of Avalon) was called Meuin. He flourished about 560. Pitsaeus names three books of his: (1) of British antiquities; (2) of the Acts of the Britons; (3) of the round table of King Arthur (Aetas 60, 560, N.50). *Vide* later, pp. 151, 159.

West Hill Hill Hill. So that the explanation just offered of the name Glastonbury is not impossible. But quite different explanations are offered. A plausible one is set forth by Dr. C. R. Davey Biggs in his *Ictis and Avallon* (where he attempts to show that Avalon is also the celebrated Ictis), and he attributes all three names, Ynnis Witryn, Avalon, and Glastonbury as derivatives from persons all members of one ruling family. He derives the name Avalon from the King Avallach, Apallach, Aballac, Avalloc, of the Grail stories and early historians, the contemporary of St. Joseph; Witryn from Gwytherin, latinized as Victorinus, a descendant of Avallach; and Glastonbury from Glast, a contemporary of King Arthur, and another descendant of Avallach. Many others have derived Glastonbury from the borough of Glastings, the descendants of Glast. Be these theories as they may, "The Mother Church of the British Isles is the Church in Insula Avallonia, called by the Saxons 'Glaston'," wrote the learned Archbishop Ussher.

"It is certain that Britain received the Faith in the first age from the first sowers of the Word. Of all the churches whose origin I have investigated in Britain, the church of Glastonbury is the most ancient," wrote Sir Henry Spelman in his *Concilia*, and again he wrote in the same work : "We have abundant evidence that this Britain of ours received the Faith, and that from the disciples of Christ Himself, soon after the Crucifixion of Christ."[2]

Robert Parsons, the Jesuit, in his *Three Conversions of England*,[3] admits that "The Christian religion began in Britain within fifty years of Christ's ascension." His co-religionist, the very learned Alford, in his *Regia Fides*[4]

---

[2] Page 1 of the folio edition. See later.

[3] First under St. Joseph; second under Fagan and Dyfan; third under St. Augustine. Vol. 1, p. 26.

[4] Vol. 1, p. 19.

says: "It is perfectly certain that, before St. Paul had come to Rome, Aristobulus was absent in Britain."

The discreet Fuller goes so far as to say: "If credit be given to these ancient authors, this Church without competition was senior to all Christian Churches in the world."[5]

"Britain," wrote the erudite Polydore Vergil, "partly through Joseph of Arimathea, partly through Fugatus and Damianus, was of all kingdoms the first that received the Gospel."[6] Polydore Vergil had special access to sources of the Glastonbury story. He was Prebendary of Brent in Wells Cathedral, and Archdeacon of Wells, six miles from Glastonbury. In 1504 he was actually enthroned Bishop of Bath and Wells as proxy for his foreign non-resident kinsman, Adrian de Castello, and acted for him. He was very critical. He rejected the stories of Brute and Arthur, and despised Geoffrey of Monmouth. But he believed in the story of St. Joseph. He was a very liberal-minded man. In 1547 he signed a declaration in favour of the Communion in both kinds.[7] He was born at Urbino in Italy about 1470. He came of a literary family for four generations. One brother was a Professor of Philosophy at Pavia; another, Jerome, was a London merchant. He himself, after studying at Bologna and Padua, and acting as Chamberlain to Pope Alexander IV (1492–1498), came to England as Sub-Collector of Peter's Pence, and for some time he led a literary life in London, and Henry VII asked him to write an English History. Such was Polydore Vergil who bore the above testimony. The testimony of a learned Italian

---

[5] London edition, 1837. Vol. 1, Bk. 1, Sec. 13, p. 14.
[6] Lib. II.
[7] Forbidden in 1175: permitted by the Council of Basle 1431 onwards. This Council tried to establish that General Councils were above Popes. Eugenius IV had agreed but it deposed him.

steeped in English history, resident in England, well-versed in the lore of Glastonbury, that England was the first country to receive the Gospel is particularly valuable.

It is a matter of distinct interest, which we commend to modern Roman Catholics, that Cardinal Pole, twice over, when solemnly reconciling England to the Pope and the Church of Rome, at the beginning of Queen Mary's reign, claimed that Britain was the first country to be converted to Christianity. Before Philip and Mary under a cloth of state, and the assembled Lords and Commons in the great Chamber at Whitehall, the Cardinal said, "The See Apostolic from whence I come hath a special respect to this realm above all others, and not without cause, seeing that God Himself, as it were, by providence hath given to this realm prerogative of nobility above all others, which to make plain unto you, it is to be considered that this island first of all islands received the light of Christ's religion", evidently confirming Gildas' statement![8]

The next day in Westminster Abbey, before Philip and Mary in state, and the Lords and Commons assembled for the act of reconciliation, the Cardinal uttered these words: "Once again God hath given a token of His special favour to the realm, for as this nation in the time of the Primitive Church was the first to be called out of the darkness of heathenism, so now they are the first to whom God has given grace to repent of their schism," etc.[9] Too many modern Catholics, and even modern Roman monks, are much too fond of speaking as if all monks were liars and inventors of fables. It does not increase one's respect for modern monks. And it may be inconvenient, but in passages like this Rome in her palmy days admitted that the British Church was at least an elder sister, certainly not

[8] Fox's *Acts and Mon.*, Vol. VI, p. 568. *Chronicles of Queen Jane*, Appendix X, pp. 154 and 13b.

[9] Fox's *Acts and Mon.*, Vol. VI, p. 572.

a daughter, of the Roman. Modern Roman Catholics are too often much more Roman than Catholic.

The Venerable Bede, writing about A.D. 740, says: "The Britons preserved the Faith which they had received under King Lucius uncorrupted, and continued in peace and tranquillity until the time of the Emperor Diocletian." That the Venerable Bede does not refer to St. Joseph is not surprising. Neither does he refer to St. Patrick. It may be pleaded that he was born and lived in the North. This would give more reason for his ignorance of St. Joseph than of St. Patrick, for the North owed so much to St. Patrick. Therefore the two silences rather drive us to Professor Stokes's explanation (*Ireland and the Celtic Church*, p. 29 note): "In presence of this notice [Cummian's reference to St. Patrick in A.D. 634 in his letter to the Abbot of Iona where he calls him 'St. Patrick, our Pope'] the silence of St. Bede about St. Patrick is of no account. He was intensely Roman, and despised the Celtic and Patrician party in England and Ireland alike." Bede's silence about St. Patrick must have been purposed. Very probably, therefore, that about St. Joseph was. And it helps us to realize how the memory of a great and flourishing Celtic Church was buried beneath the waves of heathen Saxon and Danish ravages, and the Romanizing Norman influence until it was revived in the reign of Henry II, by attention being drawn to Glastonbury and her two great stories by the discovery of the body of King Arthur.

Above are at random a number of quotations from recognized authorities of the immense antiquity and apostolic origin of our National Church, and of Glastonbury as being the Mother Church of the Island. It will be noticed that two distinct events are spoken of:

(1) The foundation of the Church in England by the Disciples of Christ.

B

(2) The acceptance of Christianity by the British Nation under Good King Lucius (Lleiver or Lleufer Mawr) about A.D. 170.

Britain was the first of all nations to accept Christianity as its national religion. Few people realize that this is why the British King is called " our Most Religious King ".

There remained for the French King the title of " Most Christian King ", and for the Spanish " Most Catholic King ". We have too much forgotten our great inheritance, which was so firmly defended by our British Archbishop and Bishops in the days of St. Augustine.[10] How many Britons realize that the superior dignity and antiquity of our national Church has been decided by Church Councils? It was never disputed till 1409 when, for political purposes, it was called in question by the Ambassadors of France and Spain, and then four times our claim was asserted at the Councils of Pisa in 1409, Constance in 1417, Sienna in 1424, and Basle in 1434.[11] It was there contended that the Churches of France and Spain must yield in points of antiquity and precedence to that of Britain, as the latter Church was founded by Joseph of Arimathea immediately after the Passion of Christ (" statim post passionem Christi "). There is a rare quarto giving the pleadings at the Council of Constance.[12]

At Pisa in 1409 the English delegates were Robert Hallam, Bishop of Salisbury, Henry Chichele (Archbishop

[10] Bede's *Ecc. Hist.* Bk. 2. Cap. 2, and Spelman's *Concilia* p. 108.

[11] Nicholas Frome, Abbot of Glastonbury, was an English envoy.

[12] *Disputatio super Dignitatem Angliae et Galliae in Concilio Constantiano.* Theodore Martin, Lovan, 1517. This book was printed through the influence of Sir Robert Wingfield, the English ambassador to the Emperor Maximilian. (Cressy's *Church Hist. of Britain*, Lib. II, p. 20.)

of Canterbury in 1414), and Thomas Chillenden, Prior of Christ Church, Canterbury. Hallam was the leader. So he was at Sienna in 1424. With him there was Nicholas Bubwith, Bishop of Bath and Wells (whose chantry is in the grave there), and the Bishop of St. David's. Cardinal Beaufort, then Bishop of Winchester, joined them later. He had been Dean of Wells. Evidently the authorities at Wells, though there was constant friction between the Abbots of Glastonbury and the Bishops of Bath and Wells, believed in the claims of Glastonbury then. Nicholas Frome, Abbot of Glastonbury, was actually one of the English envoys at Basle in 1434. The Spanish Church claimed to have been founded by St. James, the French by Dionysius the Areopagite—hence St. Denis.

The learned Archbishop Ussher recording the claims put forth by the English Church at these Councils specifically says that St. Joseph's burial at Glastonbury and the donation of the XII Hides by King Arviragus to him was the base of the claims.[13]

There are two different dates claimed for the founding of Glastonbury Church, A.D. 37 and A.D. 63. Probably both dates accentuate some special event. I will give one or two reasons for the earlier date. Gildas the Wise, the earliest Christian historian (A.D. 425–512) distinctly says that the Light of Christ shone here in the last year of the reign of Tiberius Caesar, that is A.D. 37. This falls in with the claim recorded above, which gave precedence to British Bishops at the Church Councils on the ground that Britain was converted " immediately after the Passion of Jesus Christ ". It fits in also with the statements of Fuller and Polydore Vergil already recorded (the latter a learned Italian) that

---

[13] Archbishop Ussher also refers to the two MS. transcripts of the Council of Constance, one in the Royal Library, another formerly the property of Cardinal Peter Bembi, in the private library of D. Henry Wotton. Ussher, Cap. II.

the Church of Glastonbury was the Senior Church of the world; with Sir Henry Spelman's words that Britain received the Faith soon after the Crucifixion; with Alford's statement that Aristobulus was in Britain before St. Paul went to Rome; with the observance by the Greek Church of the martyrdom in Britain of Our Lord's disciple, St. Simon Zelotes, on May 10, A.D. 44 (a date supported by Cardinal Baronius); and with Hippolytus' (born about A.D. 160) inclusion of that Apostle in his list as "Bishop of the Britons". All these are testimony to the year A.D. 37 as marking the coming of the first Mission and not to the date A.D. 63.[14]

[14] It is quite possible that St. Joseph, familiar with Britain, brought the Blessed Virgin here as her Paranymphos when St. John was at Ephesus, A.D. 37, lived with her here till her *koimesis* fifteen years later, then went to France with St. Philip, was later sent by him to Britain as a missionary in A.D. 63. (See Pynson's *Metrical Life of St. Joseph*, A.D. 1520.)